PLUMAS SKETCHES

written by
JANE BRAXTON LITTLE

drawn by
SALLY POSNER

Manufactured in the United States of America

Published by Wolf Creek Press, Box 327, Canyondam, Ca. 95923

Library of Congress Catalog Card Number: 83-050356
ISBN: 0-9611886-0-X (paper)
ISBN: 0-9611886-1-8 (cloth)

First Edition: November 1983

Second Edition: July 1984

to
Jon, Jed & Jerome
and
Rob, Dave & Sam

INTRODUCTION

Before the gold rush Plumas County had no permanent buildings, and no tales of wealth and ruin. The native American Maidus left little trace of the camps they had made for thousands of years. The infrequent trappers passed quickly along their trails, pausing in 1820 only long enough to give the county's patron river its name, Rio de las Plumas.

Then, in 1849, a man named Stoddard came stumbling out of the mountains sputtering a crazed tale— the seminal story which spawned a century of anecdotes, and these sketches. Stoddard's ravings about a lake, with chunks of gold lining its bottom, circulated among the bars from Marysville to San Francisco. By spring, over 1,000 miners rushed into the Sierra snow in hot pursuit. Their summer of diggings produced a few rich men, and a legacy of autobiographic place names — Humbug Valley, Last Chance Creek, Poverty and Graveyard flats.

Plumas County was born. Once the mineral wealth of the Feather River country was discovered, other prospectors found its rich soils, and, later, its timber and water wealth. They settled in communities near the resources, harvesting them for the beginnings of an economy based solely on what the land could produce.

Wherever they lived the settlers built cabins and halls to house their activities. The buildings presented here are a few that survived a century of life and death with stories to match Stoddard's.

Even the oldest among them is too young to have a formal, written history. All that is recorded of the dramas played out within their walls is an oral tradition, enlivened by the quirks of memory. As researchers we sneezed through the dusty editions of old news papers and everything else in print, drove back roads to visit remote cabins, and spent endless afternoons listening to the first-person accounts of these buildings' friends and caretakers. We absorbed it all, and, when in doubt, made our own best guesses as to sequences and dates.

What has emerged as "Plumas Sketches" is a whimsical outline of Plumas County's history since the arrival of the miner-settlers -- a youthful tale of adventure and hardship. As important as it is, the story of 130 years of social and architectural development in Plumas County is a slender one. Progress has done little to change the land. Mud slides still close the canyons; fires still threaten the towns; and the economy is still as dependent on Plumas County's natural resources as the first miner was on his pan.

But the stories are rich, and live on from famine to feast. These sketches are a tribute to all that is noble about Plumas County, and all that is trivial and human.

BECKWOURTH CABIN
Sierra Valley

When James Beckwourth built his first Sierra Valley cabin in the spring of 1852, he claimed it was the only building between the Feather River and Salt Lake City. A year earlier Beckwourth had crossed the 5218-foot pass used for centuries by Indians, and in the tradition of American explorers, had given it his name. He advertised Beckwourth Pass as the shortest, safest emigrant route to Marysville.

The pioneers who took his word increased each year; by 1854 over 1,200 of them had entered Sierra Valley. Although most went on to the California gold fields, some pioneers and their families settled to cultivate the soil among the tall grasses mixed with wild flowers. These early Sierra Valley ranchers were the beginning of the prosperous communities that began sprouting throughout the Feather River country. They began a new era for the territory that would become Plumas County -- an era of self-sufficiency which ended the seasonal flights to lower elevations, and the constant fear of death by starvation and exposure.

Beckwourth established his cabin as an emigrants' landing place. He offered them flour, whiskey, fresh meat and a welcome rest at his doorstep. His first and second cabins burned and were replaced in 1852 by this two-room trading post built of V-notched logs chinked with mud and small stones. Beckwourth presided over the pioneer migration from the main room by day; by night he dictated his memoirs to Squire Thomas D. Bonner. Bonner wrote it all down: Beckwourth's birth in 1798 to a Virginia slave; his early explorations with General Ashley; and his adoption by Crow Indians. Beckwourth suffered from neither temperance nor modesty, and as their late-night sessions grew longer and their rum supply shorter, Beckwourth was said to have slapped his biographer on the knee and snorted, "Paint her up, Bonner! Paint her up."

When Beckwourth left Sierra Valley, his holdings were purchased by Alexander Kirby. The trading post was used to store ice, cut in blocks each winter from the river. The property then passed to Alfonso Ramelli, an Italian-Swiss immigrant who ranched in Nevada before moving to Plumas County. The cabin served as as a milkhouse in the shadow of the great barns Ramelli built in the 1880s for his dairy operation. A frame lean-to was tacked to one side and a porch added at the rear.

With the breakup of the Ramelli Ranch

in the late 1970s, Plumas County's oldest building was left to the mice and its memories with an E Clampus Vitas plaque nailed to one weathered log.

KELLOGG HOME
Rich Bar

Rich Bar sprang overnight out of river rocks. When the snows melted in 1850, miners rushed to the banks of the Feather River's North Fork, appetites whetted by the glittering tales that Stoddard had fed them all that winter. Then a man named Greenwood pulled $2,900 in gold from just two pans of dirt, and the crowd converged at Rich Bar. By August, over 1,000 former doctors, lawyers, foreigners and school boys worked elbow-to-elbow on 40-foot square claims along a 10-mile stretch of the river.

Dewitt Kellogg was among the very few early Rich Bar miners to be distinguished by the civilizing presence of a wife. In 1853, their son Langdon was born on Indian Hill, above the huddle of trading posts, saloons and gambling halls which made up Rich Bar. Unlike the hordes who spent summers camping by the mountain streams, and winters sprawling in the Sacramento Valley bars, the Kelloggs were true residents of Rich Bar. After

enduring a variety of tents and calico-covered lean-tos, the Kelloggs built this house in 1862. They milled the lumber from a 75-acre logging grant in Kellogg Ravine. The two small bedrooms, living room, and kitchen, papered in Dresden-blue print, inspired more than one lonely prospector to leave the California adventure for his faithful wife and a roof without leaks.

In 1872, the Kelloggs sold out for $400 to a pair of French miners, Jean Lazier and Aime Lucien Roydor. The days of panning at Rich Bar had long since given way to ground sluicing. Lazier and his mining group used four-inch hydraulic nozzles on cannonlike monitors to blast the pay dirt out of the mountains. Their prospecting along Kellogg Creek stopped just short of the cabin porch, and left the house simultaneously on the brink of wealth and disaster. Lazier was joined in 1878 by his nephew, John Frank Eyraud, who left France just in time to avoid conscription in the army. Frank learned enough English to court and marry Lena Gansner, daughter

of a brewery owner just downstream.

Rich Bar was gradually deserted by miners, but the Eyraud house filled with three daughters. Frank and Lazier turned from hydraulic mining, banned in 1883, to drift mining. Around the house they created a garden spot, using a system of flumes to water a grape arbor, fig trees, pears, prunes and apples.

The fruits prospered but the planters gradually died, until by 1941 Eva, the youngest girl, was left alone on Indian Hill. As she tended the family property, with a calico cat as her sole companion, the wildlife began creeping back to the lush hillside. Eva welcomed it, limping out with aid of an old mop handle to feed the deer apples from her apron.

MASONIC HALL
Quincy

In 1855 the collection of buildings called Quincy included little more than a few crude houses, H. J. Bradley's American Ranch and public house, and a hotel at the other end of Main Street. But Quincy had been declared the Plumas County seat the year before, and in January had snatched the post office location from Elizabethtown one mile to the north.

So it was here, on Harbison Street, that the Free and Accepted Masons built their Plumas Lodge that spring. The hand-hewn pillars supported a two-story structure, enclosed by white clapboard siding bearing the marks of hand planers. The pioneer Masons mounted their emblem under the peak of the shake roof, and began meeting "on each Saturday of or the next succeeding the full moon."

Since the Masons' wives raised much of the money for the new building, they were given the use of the downstairs room. The ladies outfitted it as a school

where classes were held for 20 years. Later the Women's Christian Temperance Union conducted the county library at the Masonic Hall until it was moved in 1921 into the new county courthouse.

One of the Plumas Lodge's most distinguished early members was Thomas B. Shannon. He arrived in Quincy in 1854 as Honest Tom the Tinker. Shannon progressed from a vocation of mending pots and pans to politics. His career began with his election in 1858 to the Plumas County Board of Supervisors, and culminated in 1863 with his election to the U.S. House of Representatives.

The darkest year for the Plumas Lodge -- and for Quincy -- was 1902. Membership dropped from 54 to 17 as the town itself slid towards the oblivion that was notorious among gold mining towns. Masonic history credits the fighting spirit of Past Masters Daniel Goodwin, Arthur Keddie and the Western Pacific Railroad with saving the day. Membership increased with business brought by the new rail line, and it continued to burgeon into the late twentieth century. Modern Plumas Lodge Masons meet in Quincy's oldest building under the gaze of George Washington, who has presided in Masonic apron for 130 years from a color print in the second-floor ceremonial room.

WHEATON HOME
Taylorsville

White emigrants had come and gone, but none lived in Indian Valley on February 12, 1852, when Job Taylor arrived from Nelson Creek. Taylor claimed the land for a ranch. By fall, several families who had traveled through Beckwourth Pass collected near Taylor. His house served as a precinct for the presidential election, when Franklin Pierce carried Taylorsville as well as the nation.

Wiser than most pioneer town fathers, Job Taylor recognized the importance of good relations between the native Americans and the immigrants. In November, 1853, he convened a meeting of representatives of whites and Indians. They agreed on equal justice for equal crimes. Their pledge was soon tested. In December George Rose was found guilty of killing an Indian and was executed. Early in 1854 an Indian, son of North Arm Chief Rattlesnake, was tried for theft and was hanged.

In 1857 Edwin D. Hosselkus used lumber from Job Taylor's sawmill to build this two-story home. It stood on its rock foundation in the center of town as settlers expanded ranches, mined the surrounding mountains, and provided services to the increasing number of travelers on the road from Beckwourth to Greenville. In 1865 Hosselkus traded his house to James Wheaton for Wheaton's homestead in Genesee Valley. The Wheatons gave the house to their adopted son, Leland Pierce, when he married Juno Evans in 1897. Their daughter, Vena, was the youngest of the eight Pierce children to race the L-shape porch and carve initials in the weathered wood siding. The house stood vacant for many years, but in 1978 Vena moved back into her childhood home and began restoring it.

UNION HOTEL
La Porte

Before the advent of skiing, the most popular winter sport in La Porte was bathing in Fritz Bruhn's circular, tin bathtub. Miners paid $1.50 to soap up on the wooden seat at the tub side. On a Saturday night, a good place in line could cost up to $5.

But the long winters at 4500 feet soon produced skiing, known up and down the Sierra as snowshoeing. The world's first ski club was organized in 1866 in this hotel. The next winter, its three stories were filled with the participants, "dopemen"; and fans who converged in La Porte for the world's first downhill ski race. The annual races continued to attract crowds even after 1882, when a race entrant attired in bonnet and veil was shot and killed as he removed his girlish gear to collect the $1,000 purse.

In 1884, Francis Cayot married Claire Quigley on snowshoes and succeeded his parents as owner of the Union Hotel. The grand bar, dining room, and upstairs bedrooms had served the public since 1855 when the community known as Rabbit Creek hopped with 3,000 miners. The present building, erected in 1905, is the fifth one built in the same style on the original location. But the Cayots presided over a dwindling number of guests. Placer gold had been panned out and hydraulic mining outlawed. La Porte became increasingly removed from Plumas County activity, despite a fine wagon road to Quincy built in 1867. The hotel vault, once heavy with nuggets and sacks of miners' loot, was filled only occasionally by a traveler's jewelry.

When Francis died in 1920, his ashes were placed in the same vault to await burial with his wife's remains. For the 30 years that Claire Cayot managed the hotel by herself, the children of La Porte were spooked by the knowledge of those ashes waiting patiently in that locked corner of the hotel. In 1950, the Cayots'

urns were finally placed together in the La Porte Cemetery. Under new management, the vault's iron doors became an imposing entry to the Union Hotel.

HAMILTON MILKHOUSE
Lake Almanor

Most of the emigrants stumbling along Lassen's Trail to the California gold fields saw Big Meadows as a welcome rest stop, but to John Hamilton the 25 miles of meadow, laced by the Feather River, looked like home. He was the first white settler on the east side of the valley, building his dairy ranch in 1856 near the Maidu winter camps. Two generations of Hamilton children made play-houses in the tall grass along the river, spending summer afternoons on their backs watching bald eagles work the thermals off Dyer Mountain.

All this ended in 1901, when Great Western Power Company bought the Hamilton ranch for $50,000, a crucial first step in the creation of Lake Almanor. The family abandoned all, including the log milkhouse by the creek, where butter had been kept cool before shipment to Chico.

Fifty years later, the desolate milkhouse was disassembled, log by hand-

hewn log, and moved 50 feet upshore. By evening of the day of the move, it shone like a jack-o-lantern, its 8 by 15-inch logs still unchinked. Blanch Davis Gill and her family enjoyed the old milkhouse as a summer home until 1970, when they converted it into a country kitchen and added a house constructed of McCloud Railroad ties. The house water system was gravity fed from the creek that a century earlier had chilled Hamilton butter inside the same log walls.

HICKERSON WAGON SHED
Indian Valley

Peter Lassen made the first white settlement in Indian Valley where the lower slopes of Keddie Ridge cup the southwestern sun against the meadow. In 1851, he was selling turnips, beets and the other vegetables he raised to emigrants passing his square, log trading post. Lassen left in the fall, and the spot favored with good water and a long local growing season became the home of William T. Ward. When Ward was called off the farm to become Plumas County's first judge, Andrew Jackson Hickerson acquired the land, and he kept it. In 1983 the ranch he established was still in his family's ownership.

Hickerson's 323 acres included 70 planted in grain and 120 in hay, along with 550 fruit trees and a 30-cow dairy herd. He owned a flail, and cleaned his grain with a fanning machine which was the pride of Indian Valley. This wagon shed, built on rock cornerstones in the early 1860s, was sized to drive a loaded wagon under its cedar shake roof. One of the four enclosed storerooms in the side walls was lined with metal and used as a rodent-proof granary.

Behind the house and ranch buildings, Hickerson had a quarter-acre pond, dug by Chinese and Indian hand labor. It was shared by a school of large carp, and local members of the Immersionist persuasion, who used it to baptize their converts.

TWENTY MILE HOUSE
Cromberg

The place looked like "holy hell" in 1945 when Henry Magill ventured back to the Cromberg stage stop of his childhood. He overcame his fear of stepping on the porch and bought it -- legend, "Hobo garbage" and all. The modest trading post had been built in 1854 for local miners. Soon teamsters hauling freight over Beckwourth Pass to Quincy had begun resting there, naming it Twenty Mile House for its distance from both towns. The German pioneers William and Gerhard Langhörst bought the stage stop in 1880. They added a store and post office in a two-story annex tacked onto the original building.

Two of the Langhörsts' early customers, Ephriam C. Ross and John Crawford, were engaged in a bitter game of cards in the saloon when Ross called Crawford a cheat. Crawford shot and killed him in the very room Henry Magill later used as a bedroom. Justice was swift and Crawford was hanged. Years later a woman passing through Cromberg asked the Magills for a piece of the noose. Not wishing to disappoint her, Henry produced a section of well-used rope with which he reluctantly parted for $5.

Henry and his parents face-lifted the deteriorating stage stop with 50,000 used bricks and gingerbread salvaged from Hobart Mills. In 1983 Henry still lived there with a collection of foreign paintings, a Thai Buddha and an aging Dalmatian dog.

19

EDE HOME
Sierra Valley

The long journey across the plains by covered wagon ended in Sierra Valley in 1859 for Abraham and Mary Jane Ede. They settled on the land at the base of the "Buttes" to begin a life of dairy ranching. Mary Jane was the first white woman on the north side of the valley.

Abraham built this New England colonial-style house in 1860 for his family of 14. All of the rooms were large, but the 20-by 40-foot second-floor rumpus room was grandiose. On those rare occasions when Sierra Valley ranchers left their work to socialize, they took their families and covered dishes to Abe Ede's. The music and dancing that filled the Edes' upstairs room reverberated across the valley until the sun lit the sage on Beckwourth Pass.

In 1902, one year after Abraham died, his son William was murdered. John Mullins, a former boarder, was found guilty. During the sensational trial, the newspapers hinted at "a family row." But Mullins finally confessed that a deadly rage overtook him when William refused to let him marry his 17-year old daughter Louise. Mullins was sentenced to life in prison.

Sam Bonta purchased the 2,500-acre ranch in 1929 and continued to use Ede's fine barn and sheds. But the old house stood empty until 1945, when Sam Jr. and his wife Marie began making it habitable for their own young family.

STOVER HORSE BARN
Chester

Young George Stover left the shelter of the barn. He trudged across the packed snow pulling a sled loaded with hay. In the trees he found the cows huddled with their backs to the storm. He left the hay. It would nourish the animals until morning when he would return.

George's father, Reuben Stover, first brought his family and his dairy herd to the North Fork of the Feather River in Big Meadows in 1859. Many emigrants had crossed the Maidu camping grounds on Lassen's trail, but Reuben and his brother Thaddeus were the first to homestead there. In 1862 they built a house, barn and sheds from lumber sawn by Charlie Lawrence of Greenville and Johnny McBeth of Butt Valley. Windows and furniture were freighted in from Chico over Humbolt Summit.

Butter was the main product of the Stover ranch. Each year 7,000 pounds were hand churned, packed in firkins and insulated with hay for the three-day haul to the market in Chico. When miners moved to Idaho in the 1860s, some Stover butter went along, traveling over Fredonyer Pass to Susanville and north along the stage road to Ruby City.

George Stover's younger brother Charley continued the family ranch operation after their father died.

Each summer from 1920 to 1938, the Stover ranch was the site of the Chester Rodeo. The celebration attracted people from all over northern California, including cowboys on the rodeo circuit and local loggers. The Chester Rodeo came to feature nightly fights between the cowboys and the loggers, a tradition that was slow to die.

When the cattle operation on the Stover ranch became seasonal in 1900 the weather vane on this horse barn pointed for no one in particular for seven months of the year. But during the other five months, the barn still sheltered horses, pack gear, and an ever changing stock of cowboy graffiti.

23

DOTTA BARN
Butt Creek

Josephine Dotta had slept restlessly for weeks. The snow was nearly gone from the meadow beyond the house, and spring promised to return with apple blossoms, camas and miner's lettuce. But the four children coughed in the next room. Josephine got up frequently to fix damp cloths for their fevered foreheads -- a mother's desperate drive to save them from the diptheria which had already claimed her baby Frank seven years earlier.

It was no use. On May 17, ten-year old Chiara died. Two days later Josephine lost Nilda, 13 months. The daughter Josephine 4, was the fourth Dotta child to die, three of them within 17 days. Antone and Josephine Dotta buried them all in a family plot in Humbug Valley, four miles from their dairy ranch on Butt Creek. They could survive the long trip from Europe and the privations of winter at 4500 feet, but the Dottas were 60 years too early for the medical breakthrough which finally immunized children against diptheria.

The stoic Italian-Swiss pioneers somehow continued dairying on the 525-acre ranch they had home-steaded in 1867. The magnificent barn they had built in the early 1870s was supported by seven bents of hand-hewn timbers pegged together with mortice-and-tenon joints. Each winter they stacked hay from the wood-pegged floor to the shake roof. An L-shaped section to the north and east held milking bays for the cows. The Dottas salted away butter all through the winter to sell in the Sacramento Valley come spring.

After their only surviving daughter, Mary, married Bill Keefer of Chico in 1889, the Dotta ranch became a summer range for beef cattle. Later still it was leased to the Baccalas, the Dotta's Italian-Swiss neighbors. When Dr. Merritt C. Horning bought the ranch at an estate sale in 1980, he continued a "neighborly lease" agreement with the Baccala brothers for the use of his unfenced range acreage. The shed (on the cover) near the house was lined with bunks and bottles for the Baccala hands. Horning used a portion of the Dottas' meadow for a huge scientific garden. The forested land produced the lumber he would use for a new family home overlooking the century-old ranch buildings, while the sway-backed shed kept its watch over Butt

Creek in memory of the pioneers who built it in 1870.

PLUMAS COUNTY COURTHOUSE - Quincy

H. J. Bradley wanted it all: a new California county, the county seat, and the courthouse in his own backyard. As a commissioner for its organization, Bradley had helped create the County of Plumas with the Organic Act of March 18, 1854. To influence the election of Quincy as seat of the new county government, Bradley promised the people "a building suitable for a temporary courthouse with free use until a suitable structure can be built." What he provided was "a rude shake building" behind his American House hotel. When Quincy defeated Elizabethtown and O'Neill's Flat for the county seat, seven new county officers moved in. County Clerk John Harbison promptly moved out and headed the committee to secure subscriptions for a real Plumas County courthouse.

Construction on the public square began in 1858 under the direction of Duncan Robertson, a ship's carpenter who also built the Plumas House and fine pine coffins. The $13,485 white clapboard structure featured two-story wooden columns and a cupola. County officers moved in in May, 1859, when Plumas County recorded an official population of "4,042 people and 399 Chinese."

Sixty years later Plumas County rolled this courthouse aside to make way for a new $325,000 structure, to be built on the same public square. While Judge J. O. Moncur tried cases, and the Board of Supervisors overruled citizens' complaints in their old courthouse quarters, a classic Greek Revival structure took shape outside their windows. The exterior was reinforced concrete, finished in stucco, with Doric columns in the front. Inside, it included a 33 by 55-foot courtroom with a 21-foot ceiling for "correct acoustics." Floors throughout the 46-room building were of California marble with pink Tennessee marble trim. $5,700 was allocated for marble work in the toilet rooms, and a one-ton chandelier hung by a chain from the three-story ceiling in the courthouse foyer. Dedication ceremonies in September, 1921, featured the music of a chorus directed by Mrs. L. L. Clough and the Shriners Band of Reno. State governor William Stephens used the speaker's platform to lobby for construction of an all-weather highway through the Feather River Canyon. A barbecue, baseball game and dance followed, with Plumas House proprietor Phil Blume serving a midnight supper to his guests.

Along with county government, the courthouse held the county library in its west wing, and a stuffed bird collection in the east. With progress, the courthouse wings were eventually taken over by the recorder's office and the planning department.

WHITE SULPHUR SPRINGS HOTEL, Mohawk Valley

" The sheet music for Dvorak's "Humoresque" waited on the pianoforte in the parlor for the McLear girls to entertain their guests. Beyond the lace curtains, the road across Mohawk Valley from Truckee lay sprinkled with snow. Perhaps the stage would be late."

The dignified, red-shuttered structure at White Sulphur Springs began its public service in 1858 when Fred King opened it as a hotel. Elegant meals were served in its dining room to travelers making the three-day stage trip between Quincy and Truckee. Miners, down from their claims above Jamison on Gold Mountain, dropped their bags of gold dust in the hotel hall before climbing the stairs to sleep between crisp linen sheets. During most of its 50 years as a stage stop, the hotel was managed by George McLear, who bought it in 1867, and his daughters. While George tended to county business as the Mohawk area supervisor, Isabel, Maud and Edith suppressed their natural shyness to welcome travelers until the stage stopped coming past in 1907.

An added attraction at White Sulphur Springs was the natural hot water from springs on the hillside. In 1929, a large concrete pool replaced a small plunge bath. It was free to swimmers, who were invited to change into rented suits in the hotel rooms vacated by travelers. When Harry and Lea McKenzie inherited the hotel in 1974, they piped the hot water under the floor of the whole building which provided natural heat.

The McKenzies completely restored White Sulphur Springs, returning a Bruener's 1873 marble-top dresser and George McLear's pine wash stands to their original uses in the 10 second and third floor bedrooms. The downstairs hall and stairwell alone consumed 45 rolls of new wallpaper.

The bathroom at the top of the carpeted steps was given a Clio model stove made by Bridge Beach and Co. of St. Louis. In 1904 this stove had warmed a group of disgruntled citizens in the post office at nearby Wash. The residents were upset about their town's 13 saloons and its nickname, "Boozeville." As they sat around the little stove searching for a new name, they discovered "Clio," cast in bas-relief right before their eyes. It still names the town closest to White Sulphur Springs Hotel.

KAULBACK HOUSE
Quincy

Of all the self-reliant merchants who built Quincy from a raw, immigrant outpost into a self-respecting county seat, Charles T. Kaulback was the paragon. Orphaned at 11 in Boston, Charley answered a "boy wanted" ad and landed his first job as a store waiting boy. The lure of gold pulled him west with the crowd of other young entrepreneurs, and Kaulback arrived in Plumas County in 1853. When he established his general merchandis-

ing store on Main Street in Quincy, it was one of seven. Kaulback advertised an array of dress and fancy goods, stationery, candies, and furniture "for wholesale or retail, delivered at San Francisco prices." His store escaped the fire of February 18, 1861 -- Quincy's first major fire which destroyed Bradley's American Hotel, six stores and two saloons.

When Charley married Mary Loring in 1868, they began housekeeping in this early Victorian-style building, though it still lacked the details of interior doors and paint. Once completed, the Kaulback home sported a second floor balcony with an ornate railing over which the Kaulback girls would later lean in conversation with their friends on the boardwalk below. Kaulback's business prospered and he became Quincy's Wells Fargo agent.

In the winter of 1877 Charley took to bed with what his friends believed was a bout of rheumatism, his personal plague. To their shock, he died on January 28, leaving his widow with a $5000 Mutual Life Insurance policy.

BIDWELL HOUSE
Greenville

When Henry Bidwell wandered into Greenville in 1862, he found little more than a hotel and boarding house. A year earlier, the entire town had been flooded by waters bursting through the first dam at Round Valley. The deluge had killed Mr. Green, a clean-up miner, who gave his life for his gold pan, and, posthumously, his name to the town.

By the time Bidwell witnessed the failure of the second dam in 1863, he had acquired substantial interests

in gold mines from Wolf Creek to Indian Falls. In 1864, Henry joined with the Kettle Mining Company of London to construct a 25-foot rock and dirt-fill dam, and form Round Valley Reservoir. The success of this third dam resulted in a decade of din from water-powered stamp mills at prosperous quartz mines below.

Henry died suddenly in 1880, leaving his son Augustus a legacy of mining ventures. Of these, young Gus Bidwell salvaged only Round Valley Reservoir, forming Bidwell Water Company in 1886 to serve water to Greenville. Gus raised his family in this Victorian house. Getting to the privy up a steep flight of stairs on the hillside behind it was the childhood challenge of Gus's son Bruce. In front of the house was Greenville's Main Street, where Bruce could prospect for coins under the boardwalk. Both Gus and Bruce Bidwell kept daily records of local weather, a tradition continued in 1983 by Elmore Hunt, who moved into the house in 1946.

SUMMIT SCHOOL
Sierra Valley

Ranchers in eastern Sierra Valley took the education of their children in hand in May, 1868, and formed the Summit School District. The first students walked through the wild rye and sage to the one-room, clapboard schoolhouse to learn read-

ing, algebra and geography under the rule of Miss Jane Alexander Spoon. They ranged from first to eighth graders and supplied their own slates and sponges.

The thrifty Summit School parents were intent on getting their money's worth, and some complained that the second teacher, Miss Mary Street, compromised their children's education by crocheting while she walked between the desks. During the investigation by school board members Meade Turney and Williams Arms, both bachelors, Miss Street admitted her guilt, offering to the district her sixty yards of edging. Evidently charmed, Arms accepted the lace and got the teacher as well when he and Mary Street married in 1873.

In 1884, Summit District moved its school west to its present location near Vinton to accomodate the shift in school-aged population. Children continued attending the one-room building until 1949.

TAYLORSVILLE SCHOOL
Taylorsville

On March 10, 1864, twenty five Taylorsville girls and boys marched through the door of the little red brick building at the meadow's edge for the first day in their new school. Gurdon W. Meylert -- fresh from a failure at mining -- had opened the town's first public school the summer before, and building had begun in the fall.

The single room was Taylorsville's only school until the late 1930s. Then Marion Young Donnenwirth taught a second class at Young's Hotel built on the site of Job Taylor's Hotel.

The school sheltered its share of dead skunks and survived the other pranks of young minds, thanks in part to a neighborly stand of willows which grew a fresh crop of switches each spring.

The Taylorsville School held its last class in 1949 when it was condemned as a safety hazard. It relinquished its students to a new three-room structure and was left to silent distinction as Plumas County's only one-room brick school standing on its original location.

METHODIST-EPISCOPAL CHURCH
Quincy

The choir sang "Nearer My God to Thee;" the brass band played in full uniform, and the Reverend A.P. White prayed that the new white church on Jackson Street would serve the Christian community well. It was January 27, 1877; the people of Quincy had waited 20 years for their own church. From the days of the Reverend Pheletus Grove in 1858, the faithful had congregated in homes, halls and even the county courthouse. At the Exchange Saloon Building, the owner had allowed the church ladies to enter only after he had turned his "gay" pictures to the wall. The $2,000 building goal set in 1875 was met by subscriptions from members of various denominations as well as gentlemen "who gave their adherence to the tenets of no creed whatever."

The church coffers bulged after one Sunday collection in the 1880s. Earlier in the week the Reverend White had chatted with the owner of Quincy's largest saloon. That Sunday the gentleman

closed his bar, and led 50 customers and employees up the street and into the church. The startled pastor delivered his sermon on the evils of sin. Before passing the collection plate, the lay leader turned his back on the pulpit and whispered, "The ante is $20 for the first row, $10 for the next three, and $5 for the rest." He brought in the largest collection in church history.

METHODIST CHURCH
Taylorsville

Taylorsville Methodists built Plumas County's oldest remaining church in 1875 on land donated by Job and Sophie Taylor. Along with their prayers, the church women brought to the new chapel a Sunday School they had organized in 1864. In the late 1890s, they added a Ladies Aid Society.

The energy of these Taylorsville women created a series of cookbooks publishing local family recipes in 1910, 1922, 1967, 1976 and 1980. After 1957, the women began holding their weekly quilting and handicraft meetings in the new church social hall, built as a youth center in memory of Henry Dolphin. Working in the 1980s under an embroidered sampler proclaiming them "the piece makers", the Taylorsville sewing group continued a tradition of church fund raising along with an informal women's support group.

GOULD HOUSE
La Porte

If no one had moved it, this house would have washed away in the mud flow from hydraulic monitors blasting at dirt and gravel in search of gold. In La Porte in the 1860s a mere building, much less a humble home of wood, could not have diverted the mania for gold. But the house was carefully dismantled and rebuilt across town. During the summers, it shared a small meadow with 200 head of cattle kept by Jesus Maria Bastillos, the La Porte-Marysville packer.

In 1909, Arthur Truman Gould bought the frame and shake house for $120, rolled it back 50 feet to avoid wagon road dust, and moved in with his bride, Viola Bella Corbett. When their son Truman and his own bride, Helen Weaver, returned to the ancestral home in 1949, it had been vacant for 25 years. They found wallpaper peeling from its walls and ceilings, cracks in the windows, and an inside out-house. The traditional, wooden fire escape ladder descended from a second-story window, but even the 100-pound Helen feared it would not bear her to a safe emergency get-away.

The Goulds became part of the 15 member year-round community, which in 1962 acquired its 100-year-old birthright from the U. S. Forest Service in the form of a 57-acre land exchange. In 1983, La Porte subsisted on the seasonal business of tourists and summer residents, and thrived in the winter on the sanctity of the snow and the solitude.

CORBETT HOUSE
La Porte

The alarm sounded at noon on an autumn day in 1883. The windows of the little house on Church Street belched smoke; flames were already licking at the shingle roof. The miners who came to the rescue tried to stop the fire's spread by breaking up its fuel source with what they knew best--dynamite. The debris from blasting the house exploded throughout La Porte. Although the town had already burned to the ground three times in thirty years, in 1883 it escaped.

After the fire, the townsfolk gathered at the charred homesite. They rebuilt this frame house with bay windows in a burst of neighborly energy that required only one day. The ban of hydraulic mining that same year doused activity in the mining headquarters, and during its first 14 years, the house was often empty. But in 1897, David and Annie Corbett moved in with their four daughters, establishing a home that was still in the family

three generations later in 1983.

37

PIAZZONI CABIN
Seneca

Among the emigrants who ventured to Plumas County from the Italian-speaking area of Switzerland was the teenager, Baptista Piazzoni. He arrived on the North Fork of the Feather River in the late 1850s, when the early rush for placer gold had slowed, and miners had begun working in groups or as employees of mining companies.

Piazzoni made his own claim on Owl Creek north of Seneca. Most Italian-Swiss imigrants quickly left the rigors of gold mining for ranching, but Babs stuck with his claim. He began hiring men to help work his placer tunnel, and by 1874, employed 12 miners. They dug a tunnel into a hill, shored it with timbers, and picked free the placer gold embedded in the rocks.

In 1864, Babs felled several trees near his mine and hacked out 18-inch timbers to build this classic log cabin. Its single room had two small windows and a ladder up to a sleeping loft under the sugar pine shake roof. A path by the cabin led past a bramble of blackberry bushes and young apple trees to Owl Creek, where Piazzoni's crews sluiced out gold in the water rushing to join the Feather River.

Babs remained a bachelor, working all the time. When his Swiss Mine wasn't producing, he hired on at the Western or Dutch Hill mines. After his brother Christopher's farm was flooded by Lake Almanor in 1914, the two lived together in Bab's log cabin. By then, the Swiss was "not a very paying mine," but Babs kept picking out enough gold to live on.

Late in December, 1925, Babs didn't return from his work. His friends found his body in the Owl Creek tunnel, seated upright, still gripping his hammer in one hand. He was buried near the cabin under the trees where he had worked for over 60 years.

SCHIESER HOUSE
Indian Valley

The sun was barely cresting Keddie Point when the workers left the Schieser table for the threshing machine behind the barn. Silhouetted against the new-mown field, the long belt still limp between the engine and the funnel-shaped separator, the machinery promised to match the muscle of the 20-man crew gathered to harvest Joe Schieser's grain.

Threshing was an annual event in Indian Valley. It took ten horses to haul Joseph Peck's engine from ranch

to ranch, and six more to haul the separator. At the sound of a shrill whistle, two men traded shifts passing grain bundles, while a third fed the hopper. At the other end of the thresher, a sack holder caught the grain in cloth bags. A straw buck tossed the straw free of the machinery; later it would be spread out to dry in square stacks. When it was all over, Joe Schieser had a full granary, and the crew moved on to the next ranch. In 1877 Schieser planted 80 of his 217 acres in grain and harvested 125 tons of hay from the rest -- enough to feed his 20-head dairy herd until the grasses greened in the spring.

Headquarters for the 300-acre Schieser ranch was this rambling Gothic farm house Joe built in 1870 for his family of nine children. When the ranch was purchased in 1953 by Herman Posch, cattle trucks and winter range had eliminated the annual threshing parties. Herman leased part of the ranch for summer grazing. On the remainder he raised, "dogs, quarter horses and hell."

FLOURNOY BARN
Genesee

A fragrant cloud of blossoms greeted the stage as it pulled into the Flournoy ranch in May, 1875. The passengers stepped down to stretch after the eight-hour ride from Greenville, and to take lunch at Angelina Flournoy's table. The driver led four fresh horses from Robert Flournoy's barn at the edge of the orchard to complete the journey to Beckwourth -- a long day's ride at $6 per passenger.

The wagon road, completed in 1874, opened new markets for the fruits of the Flournoy ranch. Since purchasing the 450 acres in 1866, Robert had nursed his seedlings into the largest apple orchard in Plumas County. Now he could freight his crop to Virginia City.

Travel past the Flournoy's ranch increased with the success of the quartz mines in the 1880s and '90s. Among the miners on the road in 1892 was Joseph Cooke. He had flipped a coin at the intersection in Beckwourth and arrived in Genesee. There he met and married the Flournoy's youngest daughter, Timey. Their son Bob, born in the brick house, helped found the Indian Valley museum, and became known around the county as Mr. History.

CHANDLER HOUSE
American Valley

George Chandler was losing his hearing and feeling his age. He invited his younger brother to leave New England and join him on his ranch in American Valley. Benjamin "Frank" Chandler arrived in 1873 to begin a career as "a prosperous agriculturist with both profit and pleasure." The 431 acres Frank acquired from George were choice fields in a fertile valley. He raised a dairy herd, turkeys and sheep as well as vegetables. In 1890, his county fair rutabagas measured one foot in diameter.

Frank built this six-bedroom ranch house in 1880 of bricks fired on location by Chinese laborers. When his wife died in 1882, he raised his son and three daughters alone. The suitors who eventually came calling from Quincy were not always made welcome in the Chandler home. Andy Swingle, for one, heard Frank's heavy steps in the hall and slid to a hasty escape down a back porch roof near a second story window.

After the house was sold to Harry Johnson, the Chandler girls sometimes returned to lift the rugs in search of the rings they had hidden as teenagers. All that they found were the 1920-vintage newspapers which Lizzie Johnson had installed as pads when she recarpeted the floors.

Near the house was a small covered bridge over Chandler Creek. Benches were built into the walls; above them enameled basins hung from square nails. A round hole was cut into the bridge floor. When the Chandler men came in from the fields, they would sit on the benches and dip water from the creek through the hole, washing and waiting until the women called them in for supper.

43

OLSEN HOTEL
Chester

Nels Olsen stood in a whiteout some-
where between Prattville and his family
ranch north of Big Meadows. He was
lost, his skiis buried under a foot of fresh
powder. Nels damned the pouch of mail
on his back that had brought him out into
the blizzard. Then he burned it, starting
the warming fire that saved his life.

Nels and his two brothers grew up on
the dairy ranch homesteaded in 1859 by
their father, Peter Olsen. Their house,
built in the early 1870s beside the Red
Bluff-Susanville Road, was one of
only three in the area. Summers brought
travelers, vacationers with tents, and even
the mail to the Olsen Ranch. But when
winter closed in, they were left alone
again.

Everything changed for the Olsens
when Great Western Power Company announced its plans for a dam. The brothers
sold all but 150 acres of the 1,100 acre
ranch, some to Great Western and
some in 1911 as a subdivision

to the seasonal tent people who wanted
to build summer homes. Nels gave up
carrying mail and began converting the
Olsen ranch house into a hotel. He had
windows, furniture and green floral wallpaper for the dining room freighted from
Chico over Humbolt Summit. When water
began filling Big Meadows in 1914, Olsen's
yellow-shingled hotel stood ready for
guests. In the 1920s it housed the
over-nighters from Westwood who sought
the pleasures of Chester unavailable in
their own Red River Lumber Company
town. It flourished with the first economic stability brought to Chester in
1941 by Collins Pine Company. But
after Nels died in 1952, the old hotel became a seasonal ranch bunkhouse, and it deteriorated. In 1983
only loving hands and a million
dollars could restore it to its earlier
grandeur.

DONNENWIRTH CABIN
Taylorsville

George Donnenwirth wanted more than the life of a soldier in Chancellor Otto von Bismark's army. He left Germany in 1870 for freedom. Seven years later, he settled for a ranch along Indian Creek near Taylorsville.

Two small barns housed the Donnenwirth dairy operation, and a square stone house kept the milk cool. Donnenwirth built this four-room log cabin for his family, with an exterior stairway on the north wall leading to an open attic bedroom for the four Donnenwirth boys. One of the boys, Jake, later bought the general store in Taylorsville, naming it The People's Popular Store. Another son, John, went to Johnsville to mine; he eventually settled in Quincy where he was Plumas County Clerk for 14 years.

After George Donnenwirth died, Rufus Barnes purchased the ranch and added the rear section to the little log cabin. The strawberries Ruff raised in the fertile field between Indian Creek and the Genesee Road were coveted all over Indian and Genesee valleys. But the pride of the Barnes plantation was in even greater demand: Ruff was a bootlegger. When folks came to make a surreptitious purchase, Ruff's luscious, legal strawberries sweetened the real deal. By the end of Prohibition, Barnes's business connections with the influential and powerful of Plumas County had made him wealthy. He retired.

When Helene Page and her son Jerome bought the ranch in 1961, they found Donnenwirth's milk cans in the stone house. Ruff's still was in the barn, barely hidden under a lacy cobweb cover. The Pages used the ranch as a summer camp for inner-city youth who came to explore social values and academic programs on the banks of Indian Creek.

47

HOSSELKUS HOUSE & GRANARY
Genesee

The first batch of bricks fired for the house in Genesee was too soft. The second batch was just right, and in 1880 Edwin Hosselkus built his home of double-brick walls. Queen Anne windows caught the sun in two parlors, one for the morning and one for the afternoon. Five upstairs bedrooms looked out over the fields of the 1,000-acre ranch. With its white Victorian gingerbread and well-kept lawns, this building was easily elegant enough to house a two-term county supervisor. Although a fire damaged the Hosselkus home in 1905, the brick interior walls kept it from being demolished. Afterwards, patterned metal ceilings were installed as additional fire protection.

Hosselkus left county politics in 1888 to turn his full attention to ranching. Dairy herds grazed his lush meadows along Indian Creek, and a flume brought Grizzly Creek water to the vast vegetable garden next to the house. The strange-looking Durham shorthorn cattle Hosselkus introduced to the county were the laughing stock only until they produced the finest local herd.

This three-story granary was built soon after Hosselkus moved to Genesee in 1865. William Peters fitted the hand-hewn timbers together without nails. Wagons were driven into the top floor through a rear door. The husked grain was chuted down one floor to be bagged, and finally stored on the basement floor dug into the hillside. The Hosselkus family operated the ranch until 1948 when it was sold intact.

GANSNER HOUSE
Quincy

Florin Gansner was not a born logger. He had learned carpentry and mining since leaving his native Switzerland; he had built ferry landings on the Feather River at Rich Bar. But when the Gansners moved into this house near Quincy in 1868, Florin ran the sawmill on the property off-and-on for nine years. It was one of the handful of mills operated in Plumas County since J. B. Batch-

elder had built the first one in 1851 at Rich Bar. Florin also nurtured a large orchard, sold milk and butter, and fathered seven children.

Then, in 1877, Gansner decided to build his future on lumbering. He was a man of will. That January, while working in the woods, his ax slipped and struck him in the knee. When Gansner was carried home in a wagon, he called for a needle and thread, and stitched the wound shut himself. Now Gansner would be a lumber man; he announced plans for a new sawmill.

Lester Pelton came up from Placerville to design Gansner's new turbine. It was a hurdy-gurdy wheel of spider casting, nearly 15 feet across from bucket to flat bucket -- a precursor to the wheel Pelton would patent under his own name two years later. The wheel used the water that spilled 160 feet down Gansner Ravine to power two five-foot circular saws, cutting logs up to four feet in diameter. The new mill also had a planer.

Just before Thanksgiving, 1877, Gansner turned the water onto Pelton's wheel. The local newspaper bragged that the sawmill could turn out "almost any quantity of lumber in a little less than no time." In 1882, Gansner's was one of 11 sawmills in Plumas County -- seven powered by water, four by steam. Together they sawed six million feet of lumber and made one million shingles, all used within the county.

Gansner's son Frederick later set up a Pelton-**Doble** wheel near the sawmill and produced electricity with the same water. His Quincy Power and Light Company supplied most of Quincy's electrical needs until 1927. By then, the Gansner sawmill no longer ran, but a complete woodshop below the old mill was still powered by the water wheel system which Florin Gansner had built in 1877.

MASONIC HALL
Beckwourth

In 1910, the Hope Lodge of Free and Accepted Masons built a new hall for $7,333, from the bricks down to the handmade lectern. It was the last lodge they ever planned to build. Fire had destroyed their Masonic Halls in 1893 and 1909, forcing the members to borrow grocery stores and churches for the meetings they had held without fail since 1874.

The new Lodge attracted Masons throughout Sierra Valley and Portola. They arrived for meetings by sled, wagon and even train, walking into Beckwourth from the station at Hawley. The ground floor of the hall was first used as a community room. Behind these wood and glass doors, little girls learned to dance and little boys held their first shy hands at town parties. Later, after the Herdman family conducted Beckwith Mercantile Co. in the same space, other storekeepers came and went until 1943, when the Masons converted the first floor into a banquet hall.

MASONIC HALL
Greenville

In 1878 business was good in Greenville. Merchants John McBeth and D.D.
Compton had run out of storage space,
so they built this classic brick structure
as a warehouse. It supplied the community's two foundries, flour mill, sarsparilla
works, brick yard, wagon shop and sawmill.

That same year, a new Masonic Temple
was formed in Greenville, but the Sin-
cerity Lodge members waited until 1913
to purchase the brick warehouse for
$3,300. Three years later they engaged
in hot competition with Westwood's
Lassen Lodge for member candidates generated by Red River Lumber Company
and Engel Mine. By 1983, the Masons,
Eastern Stars, Odd Fellows and Rebekahs
had met on the hall's second floor for
70 years. The first floor offered a community banquet room used by the Rotary Club
and other civic groups.

CAPITOL SALOON
Quincy

Andrew "Doc" Hall was a slender teenager in the burly world of Onion Valley miners when a friend gave him some fatherly advice. He was too small for mining, he was told, and should learn a more suitable trade. So Doc learned gambling.

When he built the Capitol Saloon in Quincy in 1870, he provided "an orderly house with good services"—and a high-stakes back room. Hall shipped the original New Brunswick bar, still in use, around the horn to Oroville, and over Bucks Summit by wagon. The oak-framed mirror arrived separately, carefully packed between sacks of flour and sugar. Behind the etched-glass windows, the gentlemen of Quincy relaxed in leather lounge chairs, emptying Doc Hall's liquor bottles and filling his brass spittoons. In the back room, they mixed with any grub-stake miner who had the ante for Doc's table.

The Capitol Saloon gave the Quincy

Hose Company No. 1 its first test in December, 1878. The novice volunteers quickly extinguished the fire, which broke out on the bar roof and probably saved the entire town. The saloon also escaped the fire of 1934, which burned half of downtown Quincy.

Doc Hall left Plumas County in 1890 for a brief stint in Portland, returning to establish the Republican "Plumas Independent" newspaper and to serve two terms as Plumas County Sheriff. Ted Huskinson bought the Capitol Saloon in 1890 along with four adjacent Main Street business establishments, which together became known as the Huskinson Block. He "fancied up" the bar, adding dignified photographs between the round-topped windows and "well-furnished billard and club rooms." The Capitol Saloon became headquarters for "those who desire to praise the merits of the equine flesh of the county, or discuss pay gravel or quartz."

In 1905, Huskinson took in a renter upstairs. Louis Barrett established the first offices of the Plumas Forest Reserve in the two small rooms above the saloon. With only a desk and several wooden crates as files, Barrett administrated the three million acre tract, later divided into the Plumas and Lassen National Forests. Huskinson charged $15 a month rent, which Barrett paid out of his own pocket.

SHOO FLY BRIDGE
Indian Falls

Determined travelers had been crossing the ridges of Plumas County with saddle horses in summer, and dog express teams in winter. But the construction of county wagon roads, beginning in 1855, replaced these hardships with stage coaches, pulled in winter by freight horses wearing snowshoes.

The new, $20,000 public road from Quincy to Indian Valley along Spanish Creek, completed in the early 1870s, made the trip easy for anyone with $2 and a willingness to bounce for seven hours. Thanks to Shoo Fly Bridge over Indian Creek, stage passengers could even leave their shoes on.

The original arched truss bridge washed out, and in 1889 Kansas City Bridge and Iron Company built this wrought iron span on three-foot diameter steel piers. Shoo Fly bore wagons, stage coaches, then automobiles until 1938, when the Feather River Highway changed the route, and turned the trip across it into a sentimental journey for leisurely travelers.

CRESCENT MILLS SCHOOL
Crescent Mills

On New Year's Eve, 1889, the windows of this two-room school glowed against the night as ladies in lace-collared gowns and gents in white bow ties and black jackets danced in the new year. Two days later, Mr. Grout, Miss Raker, and 27 children replaced the dancers in the white clapboard school, built in 1888. The men had returned to the gold mines and ranches, the women to the chores of living in a gold rush town.

The same windows were blasted out in 1894 by the explosion of a near-by powder house, and in 1926 they glowed from the reflection of the fire that razed downtown Crescent Mills. But the building, teachers and children survived. During Prohibition, the teachers looked the other way as bootleggers cooked their mash in the abandoned tunnels of the Green Mountain Mine just up the draw. But neither explosions nor fire nor bootleggers damaged the school. It was declining enrollment that closed its doors in 1955.

OLSEN CABIN,
Chester

Peter and Melissa Olsen's ranch house got too crowded for Ed, their youngest son, so he built this cabin for himself-- a young man's retreat. Ed covered the logs with shake siding, and made it his home in the early 1890s.

When the Olsens were persuaded in 1911 to subdivide a portion of their 1,100 acres for summer homes, Ed reserved a lot for himself, skidded his two-story cabin 300 yards over from the ranch, and moved in with his family --skids and all. The skids under the logs soon rotted away, but the house on Gay Street stayed square. In 1979, its new owners began remodeling it for a summer home.

GENESEE STORE
Genesee

Edwin Hosselkus, Genesee rancher and Plumas County Supervisor, was also a storekeep. After selling general merchandise in Elizabethtown and Taylorsville, Hosselkus opened a general store in 1880 across the wagon road from his brick home in Genesee. The government established a post office there, with Hosselkus serving as postmaster until his death in 1892, when his son Frank took over the post.

When Frank retired in 1934, there were no new applicants for postmaster. Although the Genesee Post Office closed, the little store survived. As Plumas County's tofu center in 1980, it also offered its customers carob-covered almonds and organic ice cream.

PLUMAS-EUREKA
STAMP MILL ~ *Johnsville*

In 1851, mine prospectors discovered a rich quartz ledge on the 7,447-foot peak above Mohawk Valley, and changed the mountain's name from "Gold" to "Eureka." What these original nine found developed into the Plumas-Eureka Mine -- a $30 million lode and the single most prosperous hardrock mine in Plumas County. The Plumas-Eureka brought stable British investments to the rough-and-ready pickings of the miners who had swarmed around Jamison Creek and the Eureka claims. In 1871, the company's shareholders included gentlemen, spinsters, widows, army officers and ministers -- all English. By 1879, 88 stamps in two mills were crushing the ore hauled out of 62 miles of tunnel by over 175 men.

The Mohawk Mill, built in 1877, rose 72 feet in seven stories against the lower slopes of Eureka Peak. Outside, it was cheerful red board and batten with fancy white-trimmed windows. Inside, double mortice-and-tenon joints in timber beams supported a vertical mass of machinery, transforming quartz boulders into fine sand through a series of chutes, screens, crushers and stamps powered by a flume-fed Knight water wheel.

The company town of Johnsville,

laid out in 1876, augmented the usual compliment of mining town activities with skiing. The mine's cable-line tramway to the mill doubled as the world's first mechanized ski tow. At Eureka Bowl races, downhill skiers from LaPorte and Onion Valley tested their long-boards against the local competition. The winner of the February 22, 1872 race skied the 1,676-foot course in 22 seconds or 52 miles an hour.

When the rich Plumas-Eureka lode was exhausted in the 1890s, the effects were felt more in Johnsville than in London. Shareholders had doubled their investment in 10 years, but employment at the mine dwindled from a peak of 250 men in the 1880s to 10 in 1897. The life of a quartz miner had never been easy. Death from tunnel cave-in, loss of limb from stamp mill accident, blindness from diamond drill explosion -- these were the accepted risks. But economic depression created new hardships. Jack Boden, separated from his wife in order to work the Plumas-Eureka Mine, learned in 1891 of her

serious illness in New England and became despondent. His suicide by drowning in Eureka Lake symbolized the end of the great mine. The state of California acquired 5,000 acres of the old mining area, and in 1959 began restoration of the Mohawk Mill as a reminder of the genius of the quartz-mining engineers, and the courage of the workers.

EBY STAMP MILL
Belden

When the Feather River placer gold was exhausted in the 1850s, serious miners replaced the simple pan with tunnels, shafts, and explosives. Once the gold-bearing rock was mined, it was crushed by stamp mills, which broke down the rock in preparation for the mercury extraction process.

These five stamps were half of the mill at White Lily Mine, on the Feather River's North Fork. When the White Lily finally failed in 1937 after 39 crushing years, Angus Eby bought five of its stamps, and, in 1947, reconstructed the mill on Caribou Road. Pacific Gas and Electric Company relocated Eby's mill near Belden, where it stood as a tribute to those who toiled in the quartz mines, and a caution to the romantics who might be tempted.

BOARDING HOUSE
Jamison Mine

"Good treatment renders good service" was the philosophy of the Jamison Mine Company. In 1890--six years before the mine began production of gold--this boarding house offered the workers accomodations "unequalled in any mining district". They ate at the boarding house table, famous for its fine food and generous servings; they slept in iron bedsteads on spring mattresses. Even baths were provided by the Jamison Mining Company. By 1899 all company buildings were equipped with electricity, generated by Pelton wheels at the mill, and the Jamison Mine replaced the Plumas-Eureka as the leading producer of gold in Plumas County.

In May, 1906, the boarding house cook discovered a blaze in the sitting room, and called the alarm to the mine hoist, who blew the fire whistle. Plumas-Eureka workers joined Jamison employees to confine the flames and save the structure, minus a few lounge chairs and the sitting room drapes.

BIDWELL RETREAT
Chester

The procession moved slowly out of the pine grove, with a Red River Lumber cat in the lead. Behind it lurched this two-story colonial house on log rollers, with two girls--Dorothy Stover and Helen McKenzie--flitting on horseback from front to back door. Sometimes the girls left their horses to follow while they stowed away in the open doorways of the moving house, ignoring the plaster that fell in their braids and the groaning of the timbers beneath them. It took three days to save the Bidwell summer home--the retreat General John Bidwell had dreamed of--from the new flood levels of Lake Almanor in 1927.

Bidwell had always planned to build on the Big Meadows property he had purchased in 1868. After he died in 1900, his widow, Annie, completed this house. Its original stone foundation supported a grand parlor, with Annie's small, sunny library on one side, and a screened porch on the other. A stairway at the back of the parlor led to the bedrooms upstairs. Annie and her friends enjoyed the evening breeze off Big Meadows from the spacious verandas under the pines.

After Chester native Earl McKenzie bought the Bidwell house in 1925, he made immediate plans to move it to higher ground. The moving brigade crossed the Stover and Olsen ranches, ending beside the Red Bluff-Susanville Road next to the old golf course. The McKenzies rebuilt the backyard barbecue and verandas on the house, which stayed in their family until 1957 as a summer home and headquarters for the McKenzie-Stover Cattle Company. In 1983 the gabled white house was a fashionable dress shop, and a candidate for the National Register of Historic Places.

MILLER HOUSE
Humbug Valley

The driver was still harnessing the horses
for their stage haul to Chico, when a
young girl skipped out of Miller's hotel
and down the valley road to the soda
springs. She had a lemon in one dress
pocket and a small packet of sugar in
the other. The lemonade she mixed with
the natural soda water bubbling out of
the rocked-in pool was a treat she would
remember on the day-long dusty ride ahead.

The soda springs had been a gather-
ing spot for Maidu Indians for centuries
before Andrew Jackson Miller passed
through Humbug Valley in 1849, pack-
ing gear for miners. Andrew had returned the next year to homestead 2,400
acres, build a store, and, in 1860, construct a hotel just north of the springs.
The handful of ranchers and miners,
who were the Millers' neighbors in the
valley, were joined by fishermen and
vacationers who came each summer
to Humbug Valley and its town, Longville. After it became an established

stage stop on the route from Chico to Prattville, Longville included two hotels, several saloons and stores, a sawmill and a livery stable. Andrew Miller served as Longville postmaster and, for two terms, as Plumas County Supervisor.

After Andrew died in 1903, his son Frank built this grand Victorian house on the hill above the family hotel. Its first-floor bay windows gave a view of Yellow Creek meandering past the springs toward the Feather River. Frank's son Mark saw the first automobile on the Humbug Road, a 1910 Overland, from the second-floor, seven-sided tower which was his childhood bedroom. Although Oro Light and Power acquired most of Humbug Valley in 1908 as a reservoir site, a lake was never built. In 1983, the five-bedroom house maintained its vigil over a valley where fishermen still camped on the banks of Yellow Creek, and the soda pool still drained into a meadow of wild onions and dandelions.

FOREST SERVICE GUARD STATION, Long Valley

Law and order were first administered in the forests of Plumas County from the Capitol Saloon, where Louis Barrett set up an office in 1905 for the Plumas, Lassen, and Diamond Mountain Forest Reserves. Barrett began supervising the three million acres of federal land with a full-time staff of one. His major task was to run down the bogus mining claims plastered on the forest by "grafters out to get timber lands by hook or by crook."

Most notorious of Barrett's "shyster real estate operators and speculators" was H. H. Yard, president of the Butte and Plumas Railroad Company, the North California Mining Company, and a "promoter of mining and timber land deals". By 1905 Yard had over 265,000 acres of the Plumas Reserve under mineral claim. His crews were surveyors and timber cruisers, whose experience in tunnels was limited to a casual game of hide-and-seek. This cabin, built in

1903, was one of Yard's "mining" outposts, offering access to the vast stands of pine and fir between Indian Valley and the Feather River. In July, 1906, Barrett led the investigation which concluded the next summer with a favorable decision for the United States and a "hard jolt" for timber trespassers.

Yard's cabin was confiscated for federal use as a ranger station. During the summer of 1908, Barrett's seasonal staff included eight itinerant rangers who had passed the written and field exams ("Invalids seeking light out-of-door employment need not apply"). The cabin brought the luxury of a bunk, a stove and an outhouse to a ranger's routine of riding horseback through the forest between Belden and Big Meadows. In 1911, the Forest Reserve appropriated 80 acres of meadow east of the cabin, which provided ample grazing for a ranger's horse. Ranger D.A. McMillan even built a fence near the cabin to protect his animals, and to end the anxiety over horses straying off for better pastures.

The Forest Reserve abandoned Yard's cabin as a guard station, maintaining it only as a cache after 1914. As a mountain outpost it bears the graffiti of travelers along the dusty road from Round Valley to Rush Creek.

GRAMMAR SCHOOL
Quincy

Disapproving Quincy parents labeled the new, $10,000 grammar school pretentious. Its Victorian trim and spacious library were more than children needed to learn the three R's. But students enrolled, and instruction began in 1905 in the two classrooms behind the library. In the basement, a modern wood furnace supplied heat, and the lavatories offered running water--constantly: it flowed through an open culvert beneath the seats in separate girls' and boys' rooms.

Quincy Grammar, and the county's 56 other schools, were administered from the northeast corner of the recorder's office in the courthouse, where in 1887 the county had set aside space for the superintendent of schools. After voters approved school unification in 1948, the old Quincy Grammar School became the office of the Plumas Unified School District, one of the first unified districts in California.

MEADOW VALLEY SCHOOL
Meadow Valley

The flag that waved over the Meadow Valley School in 1888 was the first to honor any Plumas County school. Verbenia Phelps, age 7, had raised most of the money for the flag by soliciting donations at the Meadow Valley Hotel from the people who came to get their mail. By 1912 the students had outgrown the one-room building, so this frame school house with two rooms was built in the spring of 1914.

Community support for the Meadow Valley School was still strong in 1971, when the Plumas Unified School District announced its closure. Parents staged a week-long vigil to prevent busing the 20 students to Quincy. They failed. In 1972, the school was the site of Plumas County's first drug abuse workshop, and, later, a cooperative preschool.

PLUMAS COUNTY BANK
Quincy

Clark Lee collected $25,000 in capital stocks, rented some space in the drug store, and, in 1903, established the Plumas County Bank, Quincy's first. Although local gossips whispered about the out-of-town backing, and gasped

as the yellow stucco curves of the new mission-style building rolled out against Claremont Hill, the bank flourished. After it was dedicated in March, 1905, H. C. Flournoy received deposits behind an ornate grill in a white oak counter. President Lee and Vice-President Ted Huskinson sat behind walnut desks and authorized loans to any miner or rancher who could produce an upstanding co-signer or the appropriate collateral. From 1918 to 1932, Plumas County paid $145.56 per share of common stock and was regarded as one of the soundest institutions in the state.

In 1933, its prosperity suddenly ended. The Plumas County Bank failed with $500,000 in deposits and a capitalization of $120,000. The directors doled out ten cents on the dollar to distraught depositors, while President A. H. Bar invoked the homestead section of the civil code to save his home. In a bitter controversy, "pitting neighbor against neighbor," the bank's reorganization failed. When the doors reopened in 1936, it was as the Bank of America.

MILLER HOUSE
Quincy

The William J. Miller family belonged to Plumas County. Born in La Porte in 1865, William Miller spent his teenage

years at Elizabethtown, by then a deserted remnant of the mining community which had once vied with Quincy to be the county seat. After business school in San Francisco, Miller returned to Quincy in 1890 to became a merchant. He married Carrie Thompson, daughter of John "Illinois Ranch" Thompson. The Millers built this home on the corner of Jackson and Buchanan streets, where they lived for nearly fifty years.

Miller's Cash Store on Main Street offered gents' furnishings, candy and notions. Miller was also proprietor of the Quincy Hotel. Carrie was a school teacher and an accomplished water color artist, specializing in flowers and local landscapes. In 1911, Miller sold his store to accept appointment as state inheritance tax appraiser, a position which he held until 1944.

The Millers' daughter, Fay, bestowed her family's heritage on Plumas County. When she died in 1964, Fay left an endowment of $130,000 for construction of a Plumas County museum, to be dedicated to the memory of her parents.

MURRAY HOUSE
Greenville

John R. Murray arrived in Greenville by the midnight stage in 1877, a meager $7.50 in his pants pocket. A Scots bachelor, he hired on as a clerk in the general store, and soon was courting Laura Blood, daughter of a prominent Indian Valley rancher. J.R. built this pristine Victorian house in 1880 on the land given to him and Laura by her father as a wedding gift. While Laura raised the four children who soon filled the four-bedroom house, J.R. launched an entreprenural career which spanned 70 years.

He began with the purchase of the Greenville soda works. J.R. soon sold it to buy a shipment of bankrupt goods, purchased "at a low cost," and to start his own general store, selling dry goods, china, shoes and clothing -- "everything needed in the home". Next he opened a drug store behind the general store, and across the street, in a new brick building, he sold furniture. In 1883, Murray began selling insurance at the rear of the furniture store. For those beyond insuring, J.R. established Greenville's first funeral parlor.

J.R.'s son Kenneth and his wife Marie began sharing the family house in 1926, adding hardwood floors and a new generation of Murrays to slide down the bannister into the parlor. After J.R. died at 98, Kenneth and his own sons continued the insurance business, which celebrated its centennial in 1983.

HUSKINSON HOUSE
Quincy

Edward "Ted" Huskinson climbed from Plumas House hotel clerk to Plumas County Supervisor, staunch Republican, and Quincy's most prominent businessman. The Victorian house he built in 1893 was decorated with scalloped shingles and an incised second-story railing around the widow's walk, replaced in 1915 by a Classic Revival-style porch. In addition to his real estate and mining interests, Ted was "fond of a good horse", and served as secretary of the Eleventh District Agriculture Association.

CLOUGH HOUSE
Quincy

In 1859, Greenleaf Greeley Clough trekked 27 miles on snowshoes from Gibsonville to Quincy to defend a client in court. It was the beginning of a lifetime of public service, which included his appointment as Plumas County Justice Court Judge in 1877, his election as Superior Court Judge in 1879, and, later, his election to the state assembly. Judge Clough and his wife, Mattie Lowell, lived in this rambling frame house across Jackson Street from her parents.

LORING HOUSE (above)
Quincy

John Loring, a miner, built this Quincy home in 1882 just down the street from the Methodist Church, to which he gave 20 years of devoted service. A volunteer church janitor, wood procurer, fire builder and Sunday School class leader, Loring also donated shutters and a $200 bell for the church belfry. For his gifts of labor and love, Loring was memorialized in a church window.

STEPHAN HOUSE (below)
Quincy

Jake Stephan began his career in the transportation industry at the age of 8, when he drove an eight-horse team hauling mail and freight from Quincy to Boca. The family livery stable became a Chevrolet agency under Jake's management, and he actively promoted the $8 million Feather River Canyon highway. Jake and his wife, Louise, built this California bungalow in 1912. It later housed a newspaper, a lawyer, a cobbler, and the Plumas County Credit Union.

INDIAN VALLEY BANK
Greenville

Executive Officer Celia Chamberlain noticed the stranger in her Indian Valley Bank only after he pulled a very long pistol and ordered her into the

vault with cashiers Wendell McEnespy and Helen Largent. As the bandit walked out the door with $5,000, Mrs. Chamberlain set off the burglar alarm. When Frank Miller and Cy Hall arrived, they hardly recognized the white-faced trio that emerged from the vault.

Mrs. "Cheney" Chamberlain had started the Indian Valley Bank with her husband and John Murray in 1912. She survived the robbery in June, 1939, to later identify the bandit at the Amador County morgue. Cheney and her Indian Valley Bank also survived the depression, the only independent bank in the country to do so. She was the first woman elected president of the Northern California Bank Association, and headed its most successful bond drives during both world wars.

The copper-roofed, mission-style bank, built in 1913, was purchased by First Western Bank when Cheney retired in 1955. After Plumas County bought it for a Justice Court, deputy sheriffs used the old vault to store contraband for evidence in trials.

BUNKHOUSE
Onion Valley

Archie Post was the last miner to die in Onion Valley. In January, 1937, he was deep inside the Mullen Mine when the explosion of his partner's carbide lamp ignited a shed near the portal, choking the tunnel with suffocating smoke. The men who carried Post's body home to LaPorte battled a bitter January wind that froze a pint water bottle one of them carried in his back pocket. While burying Post they dug through 12 feet of snow, only to have their shovels strike another grave.

The Mullen Mine was finished. No miners came back to the bunkhouse, built in 1928. Post's death left it empty, save for an occasional cross-country skier climbing into its loft for a chilly night, leaving its firewood bin still bare in the morning. After 90 years as a boom-or-bust mining town, with a Main Street that once stretched across the entire 40-acre flat, Onion Valley was abandoned.

JOHNSVILLE HOTEL
Johnsville

Savo Sam Parlovich and his Slavic friends needed a place to stay. The fire of 1906 had leveled the business district of Johnsville, devastating both the sleeping and the drinking establishments of the town's predominantly miner population. Since Sam was paid in lumber for his labor at a Nelson Creek mine, he decided to build a boarding house. Nine bedrooms, two third-floor dormitories, and a dining room served the Slavonians, as did Milica, Sam's mail-order bride. The "red hotel" was covered with simulated brick made of embossed metal. It was the first building in Johnsville to boast electricity, and one of the first to add indoor plumbing to its comforts.

This carved mahogany and redwood bar was installed in the reception parlor of the Johnsville Hotel. After Pat and Larry Fites began restoration in 1974, they brought the bar back to its original location from the Canyon Inn next door. In 1983 the bar, a player piano, and the Fites's hospitality graced the parlor of the beautifully restored Johnsville Hotel.

CATHOLIC CHURCH
Johnsville

Jamison City bragged about its Teutonic belles and Sunday saloons, but on Sunday mornings in Johnsville, a string of men followed the superintendents of the Plumas-Eureka mines up the streets to church. An itinerant priest served the Catholic residents. Between his visits, the faithful took turns preaching. In August, 1900, the visiting Father began soliciting money for a church building. The following spring, this tiny wooden sanctuary with Gothic windows was dedicated as St. John's Catholic Church.

Activity at St. John's lapsed as Johnsville dwindled from a community of several hundred at the century's turn to just a few hardy souls in the 1950s. The building was condemned in the 1960s. Since then, it has watched over the Johnsville graveyard, increasingly dwarfed by the pines that surround it and the legends of its mining town past.

JOHNSVILLE FIREHOUSE
Johnsville

The flames which crept from the stairwell of the Eureka Hotel spread across the street to the post office, the saloon, the butcher and barber shops and beyond. It was 1906--not the first time fire had damaged the mining town of Johnsville. But this time the disaster was deepened by economic depression, and the widespread suspicion that the fire was caused by arson. Although Plumas County courts never proved it, most Johnsville residents never doubted it.

The ashes of Johnsville were two years old when this firehouse was built. Its iron bell offered as much protection as the hand-drawn hose-cart inside, but people felt better for its existence. Restoration in 1967 was inspired by Trigg Young, then owner of the Iron Door restuarant, and dedicated to the memory of his wife Jackie.

CLINCH HOUSE,
Quincy

William Clinch wanted more than prosperity: he wanted the American dream. From the time his father had acquired 100 acres in 1872, the Clinch ranch east of Quincy was known as the showplace of American Valley. The Clinchs raised cattle and hay, and William and his brothers and sisters were well fed from the vegetable garden.

The family continued to prosper. In 1905, William built the Plumas Meat Market on Main Street in Quincy, with gold-embedded rock on its walls. Here he retailed the products of many valley ranches, including his own. In the ballroom upstairs the Quincy Band held its first practice session in 1905. William's son, Brigadier William Clinch, made his own contribution to the family's achievements by composing the United States Air Force song.

But all this wasn't enough, so in 1917, William Sr. was one of 100,000 Americans who bought the kit form of the American dream, gambling on Richard Sears' pledge, on catalogue page 594, that the mail order firm could make him more of a home owner for less. This two-story, nine-room concrete block residence cost Clinch $2,200. For $782, Sears delivered the plans, the Fillmore front door with beveled glass, the finish lumber, pipe, gutter, and sash weights. Clinch also ordered a matching concrete block garage.

The house was as solid as Clinch

could have dreamed. It emerged unscathed from a 1960s fire -- set deliberately to test its strength, according to rumor -- and after 50 years looked as handsome as the day it was built.

WESTERN PACIFIC HOSPITAL
Portola

When Western Pacific Railroad construction crews arrived in Headquarters in 1906 to build the east-west Feather River Canyon line, not a solid roof protruded from the logging camp on the Middle Fork of the Feather River. W.P. set up its commissary among the tatter of tents beside the parallel tracks of its competition, the Nevada-California-Oregon and Boca-Loyalton railroads. The community grew with the railroad. Between 1906 and 1908, it was renamed Mormon, Reposa, Insola and, finally, Portola, after the daughter of W.P.'s chief engineer. who was 1908 queen of San Francisco's Portola Festival.

Before its first passenger train steamed through Portola in August, 1910, W.P. had begun construction of a hospital on the hill above the tracks. There the company cared for its employees as the town developed into Plumas County's only incorporated city. When W.P. announced plans in 1963 to close the facility, a "Save the Hospital League" kept it running for eight more years, ignoring official condemnation. When it was finally abandoned in 1971 for a new, 34-bed district hospital, the old W.P. building was remodeled into apartments for tenants who hung their wash between the emergency wing and the administration office.

RESORT CABIN
Keddie

The town of Keddie was a muddy, intemperate construction camp in 1909, when the east and west gangs met a mile down the tracks to drive in the golden spike.

The completion of Arthur Keddie's 42-year dream—a rail line from Salt Lake City to San Francisco—gave his namesake new airs. Robert Koonter bought the Utah Construction dormitory, added a general store, and got a post office registered in 1910. A year later, Charles Rehms took over with his own dream of building a railroad resort.

Rehms constructed a lodging house across from the original dorm and log cabins along the hillside between the tracks and Spanish Creek. He welcomed city vacationers, who could step down from the train into a mountain paradise for only a little more than the price of a ticket. At Keddie they could hunt, fish, and, from their stools at the Back Door Bar, practice target shooting at the empties tossed into the crawl space where the back bar should have been.

Although none of the cabins built by Rehms burned in the fire which razed the lodge in 1937, the town languished in the next decade as railroad vacations dwindled. By the time the California Zephyr made its last Feather River Canyon run in 1970, Keddie was being resettled by long-haired emigrants of the urban establishment, who planted tiny gardens in the rocky soil around the cabins and hung tie-dyed curtains in their windows. Under new ownership in 1978, Keddie was restored as a lodging and dining resort. Its first guests were 56 Japanese students, visiting Plumas County on a cultural exchange through Feather River College.

FEATHER RIVER INN
Blairsden

"To you who live in the cities, the high Sierra is calling you to come away from the moist salt air of the seashore or the enervation of the valleys...from the noise and confusion of the city with its unceasing business cares and social elements. Answer the call of the mountains in Feather River country at Feather River Inn."

At Feather River Inn you could have your country and your comforts, too, for $25 a week. In 1915, the $350,000 resort built by Van Noy Interstate Company of Chicago was the most exclusive hostelry in northern California. Travelers stepping off the Western Pacific Railroad to the tune of a brass band were jitneyed across the road, and through the stonework gates of the inn to the fully electric chalets, replete with sun parlors, fireplaces, hot and cold running water.

The inn itself was an enormous wooden building on a grassy knoll offering a dining room, lounge, assembly room, kitchen, office and sleeping apartments. Other amenities at Feather River Inn included a picture theatre, dance floor, swimming pool and tennis courts. Motor cars were available for the more adventurous hunters (limit: two bucks) and fisherman (limit: 50 fish or 10 pounds and one fish). A full-time nurse was on hand to care for the children.

Feather River Inn served fresh butter, milk and cream from its own dairy one half mile down the road. Its farm produced vegetables, poultry and beef. An electrical plant lit the verandas for midnight dancing, and an ice plant kept the champagne cold through the summer.

In 1970, the inn's 30 buildings and 100 acres were purchased by Feather River Preparatory School. This main building was converted into a high school library, student store, housing and dining area for 30 boys and 30 girls. The University of the Pacific bought the school in 1977, and continued to operate it as a prep school.

INTAKE TOWER
Lake Almanor

The 50-square miles of placid blue that are Lake Almanor began in 1901 as a "top-secret diplomatic mission." An agent for Great Western Power Company arrived in Big Meadows that fall to begin milking the dairymen of the property they had ranched for over 40 years. Innocent of any suspicion that their prosperous homes and barns, and the entire community of Prattville, would soon give way to a grand hydroelectric power scheme, they sold out one after another.

Gus Bidwell's breakneck race to the Plumas County Courthouse in 1902 gave Great Western a 40-minute advantage over the competition for Feather River water rights. Although construction of a multiple-arch dam was abandoned in 1912 amid public controversy about its safety, building immediately resumed slightly upstream. In June, 1914, an earth-fill dam was completed, extending 650 feet across the Feather River canyon

and cresting 72 feet above the stream bed. Guy Earl, Great Western's first vice president who conceived and co-ordinated the power project, named the new lake "Almanor", for his daughters Alice, Martha and Elinor.

Lake Almanor's storage capacity increased in 1927, when a higher fill dam was added just below the original one by

91

Pacific Gas and Electric Company, new owner of the multi-million dollar water power generation project. A second enlargement in the early 1960s created the present 28,000-acre water storage reservoir for seven power plants on the Feather River.

POWER HOUSE & LODGE
Caribou

In 1919, the prospectors along the North Fork of the Feather River were a new breed of miner -- hydroelectric engineers looking for the lucrative "white gold" in the water which rushed from Lake Almanor toward the Sacramento Valley. One of their principal tools was a steel, reinforced concrete structure (see page 91), the second power house constructed on the Feather River by Great Western Power Company. In 1921, its three generators began turning out 73,000 kilowatts to light homes in the San Francisco Bay Area.

The pioneer construction of Caribou No. 1 attracted mining engineers, who traveled from all parts of the world up the North Fork gorge on a cliff-hanger rail line to Caribou. Specially designed penstocks, assembled in Germany, handled the water's unusually high head, a drop of over 1,100 feet. Gravity and pressure tunnels brought water from the main reservoir at Lake Almanor down to Caribou, where 30,000 horsepower impulse turbines and an Allis Chalmers needle valve system helped the water churn the darkness to dawn.

The Caribou labor force moved from a construction camp into California-bungalow-style residences, built against the canyon above a rock retaining wall. Great Western created Caribou's first school in 1923 by offering naturalization classes to Russian workers in an electrical workshop. By 1939, the community had dedicated a new school house, where portraits of George Washington and Abe Lincoln cast stern eyes down on small desks, and waist-high hooks in the hallway received the hats and jackets of students rushing into the classroom.

In 1926, Great Western built this rustic lodge with a spacious lobby and dining room, and private bedrooms upstairs. Designed for bachelor employees, this elegantly appointed building more often housed the distinguished visitors to Caribou invited by Pacific Gas and Electric Company, its owner since 1930. Among the guests was former President Herbert Hoover, who in 1933 met there with Caribou executives and school children.

CAMP PRATTVILLE
Lake Almanor

The first ground broken in the new Prattville was for the cemetery. It was to be the final resting place for the earth-encrusted boxes transferred from the original plot in Big Meadows before the lake started to fill. Most of the rest of the pioneer community of Prattville burned during the July Fourth, 1910, baseball game against Greenville, easing Great Western Power Company's acquisition, from die-hard land owners, of the last of the ground to be submerged by Lake Almanor.

As the waters rose, the new community grew. In 1927, Frank and Mettie Wilson added to it with 10 cabins skidded to the new shoreline from Butt Lake Road, where they had been built as worker housing for the Almanor-Butt Lake tunnel construction crew, and later used by Plumas County Road Department workers. Wilson set two cabins together as a store and office. The others he rented for two dollars a day to fishermen who came for the trout that had made the original Prattville famous. Wilson also built wooden boats which were available to his seasonal guests. Under the management of Wilson's son, Ken, and his wife Carol, Lake Almanor's second resort expanded to accommodate recreational vehicles and a cafe famous for Sunday brunches and home-style dinners.

PAXTON LODGE
Paxton

Late in December, 1852, Mr. Bain left his partner at Soda Bar on the Feather River to guide three other miners to Marysville with gold for deposit. His four-day struggle through waist-deep drifts and a blizzard ended near the ruins of Rock River house. Bain died on a snow bank, cradled by a companion.

Over a century later, when Feather River College students began boarding at Soda Bar, the ghost stories which had haunted the place since Bain died were retold with fresh details. The tales hovered around the four-story lodge, built in 1917 by the Indian Valley Railroad Company. The company which hauled copper out of Engel Mine, had made Soda Bar its headquarters, renaming it Paxton after the mine's general manager. The lodge flowed with overnight guests and liquor until 1930, when copper prices crashed and Engel Mine closed. Forty years later, the students often saw the lodge lights pop on and off without explanation. They whispered of a fading presence in the rocking chair, and a partner who had disappeared. To the believers, the Paxton ghost may be the memory of all the miners — gold and copper — who rested there before moving on down the canyon.

MILL MANAGER'S HOUSE
Graeagle

The day the boxcar of grapes came to Graeagle, the people took off their shoes. Manager Herb Rowe closed the mill, the Italian workers went to mashing, and an entire logging community defied Prohibition. What they bottled was passed to underground storerooms through trapdoors in the bedrooms of the company houses.

Graeagle had been born suddenly in 1919 when Arthur Davies rolled 92 house halves from a fleet of flatbed rail cars. Reunited, the 46 houses became Davies Mill, an independent lumber town on the banks of the Feather River's Middle Fork. The California Fruit Exchange bought and renamed the town in 1921. For 36 years it ran a self-sufficient community which included a lumber mill, molding mill and box factory. At its peak, Graeagle turned out 100,000 feet per day of molding, upper-grade lumber and box stock.

In 1958, a year after the Fruit Exchange shut the mills and closed the town, Harvey West and his sons bought the 7,000 acres of timber, town, swamp and meadow for a model planned resort and retirement community. Harvey Jr. chose the vast peat bog behind the old mill for Graeagle Meadows, an 18-hole championship golf course. The locals who watched the construction of the number ten fairway remembered the tale of a man, horse and wagon that had disappeared while crossing that swamp. The designers ignored it--until a backhoe unearthed an old wagon tongue.

Harvey West, Jr., and his family lived in this mill manager's house for several years before building a new home in the Graeagle development.

DAIRY HOUSE
Graeagle

Employees of the California Fruit Exchange rented company houses for $15 a month. They ate company meat, and drank company milk from bottles whose cardboard caps read "Graeagle Lumber Company Raw Market Milk". The Fruit Exchange even piped steam heat from a central plant into its employee houses.

This stone structure built in 1921 housed the company dairy operation. It was outfitted with hot and cold running water and a shower for the milkmen. Across the meadow was the slaughter house where the Graeagle Lumber Company beef were prepared for the workers' tables.

UNION HALL
Sloat

The independent union at F.S. Murphy's sawmill in Sloat took over this club-house just after the company built it in 1918. Under Murphy's management the old Sloat mill acquired new band saws and a planer. Under the new workers' organization his employees acquired wage contracts and decent benefits.

The Sloat mill union negotiated with three separate companies before joining other Plumas County millworkers in 1963 in the Lumber and Sawmill Workers Local 3074. But when Sierra Pacific bought the mill in 1976, its new employees-- drawn into a strike within weeks of starting to work--successfully petitioned to decertify the union. With the union gone, S.P. decided to tear down the old hall. The town rallied around it, redec- orating the spare meeting room for "The Last Tango in Transylvania-West", held on Halloween, 1981. The fund raiser saved the union hall for CPR and Jazz- ercise classes, and "whatever the kids decide to put on in there."

CHESTER LIBRARY
Chester

Melissa Baily Olsen loved books. She brought precious few along on her covered wagon journey from Ohio, but she instilled her interest in literature in each of her six children and in her granddaughter Edith Martin, all raised on the Olsen dairy ranch near Big Meadows. The books Melissa managed to collect formed the first library in northern Plumas County. It moved as it grew, from Stover's general store to Maud Gay's post office.

When Edith Martin donated a generous acre of land for a library building in 1928, the community rallied 'round to build it. Fletcher Walker of Red River Lumber Company contributed the logs, and dances held in town, by then called Chester, raised money for the rest of the materials. Charley Yori and Melissa's son, George Olsen, did the inside finish work, and the Chester library opened in 1929.

During the 1940s, when Collins Pine's prosperity put Chester through growing pains, school classes met among the

books in the library by the Feather River. In 1983, it was one of four Plumas County branch libraries and bulged with over 8,400 volumes.

CARMICHAEL HOUSE
Lake Davis Road

Roy Carmichael worked against the cold to harness his team of Percherons. The pale afternoon sun hung just above the snow when he finally drove them out of the barnyard, pulling a bobsled laden with hay. The sled runners squeaked in the ruts, still solid from the morning run, as Roy drove to the upper pasture, where several head of hungry cattle waited among the belly-deep drifts.

Carmichael had purchased the old Smith ranch and adjacent lands above Portola in 1935 -- 5,000 acres for $50,000. During his first eight years there he wintered his herd over, storing some of the more than 400 tons of hay he raised in the big barn, and some in stacks in the fields.

In 1944 Roy made his first cattle drive to Vina, where he had acquired a winter ranch. The 10 day trip took him past Walker Mine into Genesee, across Indian Valley, up to Deer Creek, and finally down the old Lassen Trail to the Sacramento Valley. While other Sierra Valley ranchers used railroads for their seasonal exodus, Roy figured the drive saved him $1,000 over shipping the herd.

Roy ran the ranch from this house, built in 1935. In 1978, when he was 82, he was the last of the Sierra Valley ranchers to give up cattle drives for trucks.

NOBLE BARN
Sierra Valley

This barn near Beckwourth, built to hold hay, withstood a century of changes in the Sierra Valley economy -- but barely. For years it functioned as the winter store for cattle on the Landers ranch. In 1920, Wendell Philucius Hammon -- "that gold dredger fellow from Oroville" -- bought it, along with other Sierra Valley properties he never lived on. When Hammon's fortunes faltered with the depression, two of his losses were the gains of Edward Noble, a self-made rancher from Gerber. Noble acquired Hammon's 2,440-acre ranch outside Beckwourth in 1931, as well as his Clover Valley spread.

Noble divided his properties in Plumas and Tehama counties into summer and winter ranges, so he had no need of the barn to store hay for winter feed. When he stopped driving the cattle to the Sierra Valley summer range and began hauling them by train, Noble used the Beckwourth ranch to rest his herd after the 15-hour ride from Red Bluff. The pastures provided feed for the cattle until they could be moved to Noble's lusher Clover Valley range.

But the barn was obsolete. Sun filtered through the missing roof shakes onto empty lofts once crammed with a winter's supply of hay. The hand-hewn timbers, that had stood since the dairying days of the 1870s, groaned with the wind, and each successive winter became a test of the barn's survival.

WESTERN PACIFIC DEPOT
Greenville

The town hadn't seen such hustle since the quartz mines petered out. Just the talk of a rail line, from Keddie to Bieber through Greenville, produced Greenville's first pharmacy, a volunteer fire department, and a new, $50,000 modern hotel--all before a single tie was laid.

When the first Western Pacific train steamed through town on October 21, 1931, Greenville also had this $10,000 railroad depot, with an apartment upstairs for the agent. Downstairs a warehouse stored freight, from dry goods for Ayoob's Department Store, to boxes from Setzer Box Mill. Passenger service was never formal, but commuters to Westwood could pay the brakee to ride in the caboose. In the winter, ski excursion trains formed in San Francisco and passed through Greenville, picking up passengers headed for slopes near Bieber.

Completion of the Feather River Highway cut deeply into W.P.'s freight traffic, finally forcing the last agent to lock the doors of the Greenville depot in 1951.

HIGHWAY FOUNTAIN
Paxton

The Feather River Highway was completed in August, 1937--the final wedge in the mountains of Plumas County first cracked by miners in 1850. Billed as a snow-free, low elevation route across the Sierra, the highway included 11 bridges and three tunnels between Oroville and Keddie. Construction cost $8 million.

Among the construction crews was a gang of trustee inmates of San Quentin Prison, camped south of Paxton in 1929. Their camp water was a spring on the hill above the Feather River. In a spurt of creativity--inspired more by their relative freedom than a belated sense of civic responsibility-- the inmates built this stone fountain. Highway travelers could enjoy the cold spring water, thanks to trustees J. Vasquez and S. Chiritescue, who inscribed their names for Camp 16.

MT. HARKNESS LOOKOUT
Lassen National Park

The stone and wood tower that hunkers at the top of Mt. Harkness, at 8,045, is that rare result of a bureaucrat's paperwork. In 1930, H. E. Williams, field representative of the Secretary of the Interior, reported that fire had consumed 1,600 acres of Lassen Volcanic National Park that season. The next summer, Park Service crews packed in concrete, peeled logs, and glass for the two-story building to house a seasonal fire lookout. Mt. Harkness was the first Lassen Park operated lookout tower. It doubled as a seismographic station and a viewing point for hikers.

In the 20 years after the construction of Mt. Harkness Lookout, Lassen Park averaged only six fires per year, each one under one acre. How was Williams to know?

The lookout was manned until 1980, when reduced appropriations and cooperative fire fighting agreements with Lassen National Forest left the wooden shutters closed year round.

CHENEY STUD MILL
Greenville

The nation was gearing up for World War II when Ben and Frank Cheney began building their Greenville sawmill, the fifth one owned by the Tacoma, Washington, baseball tycoons. The Cheney Greenville plant would produce railroad ties from the Dougfir that covered the slopes of the Wolf Creek Timber Company holdings.

Slim Malvich hauled a section of a Red River Lumber Company mill down from Westwood. Bill Hall built onto it, and in June, 1941, 30 men went to work on three saw rigs. Cheney advertised it would cut 40,000 feet a day with two shifts. When the demand for rail ties ended with the war, the plant converted to a double-cut band mill for two-by-four studs.

After 33 years of stable production, the Cheneys sold their mill to the Louisiana-Pacific Corporation in 1974. L-P installed a quad mill for small logs, hauling larger sawlogs to the Crescent Mills plant it had acquired a year earlier. The 75 employees worked on the promise that the mill would stay open if production stayed high. But an average of 130,000 feet a day wasn't enough. L-P announced the mill's closure in August, 1979.

The company auctioned off the mill equipment, then donated a portion of the land to the Greenville community for a park. Ray Alves bought the balance of the property for a wood salvage operation, packaging cull logs for sale as firewood in Los Angeles.

COLLINS PINE CHATEAU
Chester

Truman Collins dreamed of a timber tract that would produce lumber perpetually. He envisioned a small sawmill offering economic stability to a mountain community, while the land was allowed to continue its own natural reforestation. His eccentric grandfather--"Teddy the tither"--had combined business savvy with Methodist piety to establish a family lumber industry worth millions. When the Pennsylvania-based Collins company began logging its holdings near Chester in 1941, Truman decided to experiment with the 90,000-acre Almanor Forest.

One of the first houses built while the Chester Collins Pine mill was still under construction was this four-bedroom residence, affectionately called "the chateau." Knotty pine paneling for the living and dining rooms was specially selected from lumber produced at the Collins plant in Pondosa.

The chateau was a guest house for Truman Collins and his brother-in-law, Elmer Goudy, during their frequent visits from Collins headquarters in Portland, Oregon. It also served as a temporary residence for mill superintendents until they found housing for their families in Chester. After the Collins Pine mill settled into steady production of 40 million feet a year with 178 employees, the management staff held meetings every Thursday noon in the chateau.

Truman's dream was kept alive by Collins's foresighted logging practices, which included natural reforestation using selected seed trees. When other private and public forest managers turned to twentieth century herbicides, Collins relied on centuries-old uneven aged management and cleanly avoided the controversy.

As the Collins sawmill entered its fifth decade of lumber production in Plumas County, some of its timbered stands had been logged three times. The tract was still supporting a mill and a stable community, and exceeding even Truman Collins's dream by producing well over 25 million feet of timber each year.

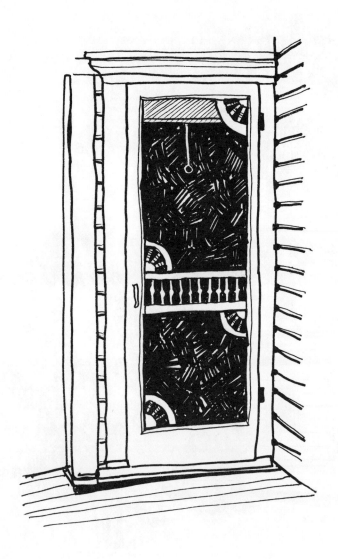

ACKNOWLEDGEMENTS

For every building in this book, there is a crew which helped raise its story. These people shared with us their enthusiasm for Plumas County's past as well as their memories and family records. Without them, this book would be little more than a wishful thought.

Our thanks to Linda Brennan and the generous contributions of the Plumas County Museum; to Bob Cooke and the Indian Valley Museum; to Marilyn Morris and the Chester-Almanor archives; to Chuck James and the U.S. Forest Service; and to the Plumas County Historical Society.

The book took a lot of help from our sons, Jed and Jerome, David and Sam, and our husbands, Jon and Rob. As production crew they photographed, traveled, edited, promoted, encouraged and assured. Our grateful appreciation to each of them.

ALSO THANKS TO:

Roy Alves, Angie Adrien, Floyd Austin, LeRoy Austin, Barry Bailey, Tim Beem, Bruce Bidwell, Perry Blake, Marie Bonta, Howard Boyer, Betty Bridgman, Ed Brown, Bill Burford, Father Bernard Burns, Roy Carmichael, Don Carr, Jay Chew, Collins Pine Company, Chuck Clay, Tamara Conner, Henry Cooley, Wayne Dakan, Waynette DeBraga, Florence Dedmon, Ray Donnenwirth, Dr. William Dore, Cal Dorithy, Betty Elledge, Amy Fendley, Larry and Pat Fites, Joeana Frantz, Len Fulton, Blanch Davis Gill, Bob Gott, Charles Goubert, Helen Wearer Gould, Billie Gronvold, David and Gretchen Groot, Alta Hall, Cy Hall, Wes Harberts, Eathel Hargraves, John Hart, Tom Hervey, Pick Hobson, Bill Hoffman, Les and Barbara Hogaboam, Dr. Merritt C. Horning, Bill Hosselkus, Elmore Hunt, Richard Kingdon, Rachael Kohler, Lassen National Park, Helen Lawry, Mike Lazzarino, Ernie Leonhardt, Doris Livingston, Henry Magill, John Malarkey, Buster and Margaret Mason, John Masson, Orma Mathews, Karen McElroy, Lea and Harry McKenzie, Mark Miller, Peter Moale, Marie Murray, Inez Nelson, Pat Noble, Claire O'Rourke, Dick O'Rourke, Pacific Gas and Electric Company, Helene and Jerome Page, Joe Palazzi, Plumas-Eureka State Park, Hattie and Harry Posner, LeRoy Post, Ron Pound, Mary Rehwald, Don Rumsey, Ron Schwartz, Michael Selic, Norm Shelton, Dr. Jerry Simison, Lillian and Warren Simison, Vena Thompson, Ken Tweeten, Richard Vance, Lucy Vernazza, Rosie Walker, Al Wellenbrock, Dan West, George Wilson, Ken and Carol Wilson, Mike Yost, and Helen Martin, who quietly renewed our overdue library books, and Valari Van Valkenburg for proofreading.

INDEX